# GREECE
## LAND OF MANY DREAMS

Text by Rupert O. Matthews
CLB 1241
© 1985 Illustrations and text: Colour Library Books Ltd.,
Guildford, Surrey, England.
Text filmsetting by Acesetters Ltd., Richmond, Surrey,
England.
Printed in Spain.
All rights reserved.
1985 edition published by Crescent Books, distributed by Crown Publishers, Inc.
ISBN 0 517 462907
h g f e d c b a

# GREECE
## LAND OF MANY DREAMS

Text by
**Rupert O. Matthews**

Foreword by
**JOHN CARTER**

**CRESCENT BOOKS**
**NEW YORK**

# FOREWORD
## by John Carter

"Of all holiday and travel memories, none is more evocative than that of a sun-drenched island rising from the calm sea upon which one sails towards it. White houses dazzle the eye as a village scatters its way down a hillside, threading among the olive trees towards a waterfront busy with small craft. Closer, one sees there are bright awnings over the quayside restaurants, with chairs and tables scattered out onto a wide promenade. The strollers pause and gather to watch the arrival of the ferry. There is noise and bustle as ropes are thrown and hauled and tied, as gangways are heaved into position, and the travellers move in or out of the scene."

I wrote those words shortly after returning home from my first visit to Greece, and know that for many people that description could fit nowhere else on earth but those islands which beckon from the wine-dark seas. When I consider which aspect of Greece has the greatest appeal, it is to those islands that my thoughts turn. Enthusiastic friends tell me that the very best type of holiday is one which has you sailing among them, perhaps independently or perhaps in convoy. I know that 'flotilla' sailing is becoming more and more popular, but have to accept the assurances of those enthusiasts, for I am not a small boat sailor. I take my islands slowly, and journey between them on the passenger ferry services.

The lure of those islands draws millions of visitors to Greece every year. So does the lure of history, and whenever I hear the phrase 'Classical Greece' or 'ancient Greece', the image that springs to mind is of scattered stones and tumbled columns on some venerable site. I don't like it when people refer to such locations as 'ruins', for the implication then is that the sites have nothing to offer us but broken remnants of the past.

For me, such places as I have visited in Greece are more like history's bookmarks, indicating a place where a great civilisation once flourished. The visitor to Greece should use such places as fuel for the imagination; to look at the stones, to listen to their story and, hopefully, to learn more about the Greece that used to be.

Whether it is your intention to hop among the islands or to visit ancient sites, to enjoy the simple pleasures of the present, or to explore the glories of the past, Greece awaits your pleasure.

*John Carter*

Exactly why the Greeks came to settle in Greece three thousand years ago nobody is quite sure; but they did and that single fact has had more influence on Western Civilisation than perhaps any other.

The first traces of the Dorians, the ancestral Greeks, are to be found along the Danube, where archaeology has turned up numerous articles of Doric culture. The Dorians were a group of warlike tribes and the reasons for their subsequent movements are obscure, though they may have been suffering attacks from other tribes. Moving up the Morava, the Dorians crossed the mountains into northern Greece and thence, around 1100 BC, past Attica and the Gulf of Corinth into the Peloponnesus. Here they found a deserted and desolate region.

At Mycenae, near the head of the Gulf of Argolis, the newcomers found the massive remains of a beautiful city, the citadel fortifications of which still stand. Walls encircle the acropolis to a height of 35 feet and are, in places, 46 feet thick. The great glory of Mycenae is the Lion Gate, which forms the main entrance. The opening is ten feet high and ten feet broad and is topped by a triangular slab of limestone of equal size, on which are carved two massively majestic lions. The sheer scale of the walls and the enormous blocks of rock from which they are constructed convinced the Dorians that no human could have built them. Mycenae, and other similar cities, were ascribed to the legendary Cyclops.

The great walls were in fact the flowering of the Aegean civilisation which had been developing in the area for a thousand years. Why such an apparently successful civilisation should disappear has been puzzling scholars ever since its discovery last century. Evidence of a widespread drought has been cited to explain the disappearence of an agricultural civilisation, while the fact that many Mycenaean cities were destroyed by fire indicates a more violent end. Civil war and revolution have both been suggested at times for the demise of the Aegean society, but it is also possible that the advancing Dorians destroyed the cities.

Having spread across the Greek peninsula, the Greeks settled down and began to build a culture of their own which would become the grandest in the world. During the first three centuries of their settlement in the peninsula the Greek tribes underwent a remarkable social transformation which had as much to do with the landscape as with themselves. Greece is characterised by small plains divided by steep mountain ranges, which in itself favours political fragmentation. The Dorians had moved south in tribal groupings and it is more than likely that each of these settled in its own area and retained its independence. Warfare was endemic, so a fortified citadel into which the population could retreat was indispensable. The citadel grew into a city upon which the surrounding agricultural land was dependent. It was probably in this way that the *polis* came into being.

The *polis*, or city state, remained the basic unit of Greek society for more than a thousand years and seems to have been the only scale at which Greeks were able to organise themselves. The *poleis* were not, however, internally stable and throughout the Archaic period, up to about 530 BC, they underwent a series of transformations. The early tribal society was not suited to a settled urban existence, nor to the citizen armies that were needed to support the hoplite phalanx. There was much unrest within *poleis*, which was often only ended when a tyrant seized power. These tyrants were far from despotic rulers and usually carried out much needed reform. Such reorganisations within the city led to the passing of the tyrants and the establishment of a form of democracy in most *poleis*.

The other great movement of the Archaic period was that of colonisation. Growing populations in Greece meant that the limited arable land could no longer support the numbers of citizens and this led to large-scale emigration. The islands in the Aegean had long been settled, so those in search of land had to travel further afield. The indentations of the Greek peninsula had led to the Greeks becoming excellent seamen; a fact which was exploited by colonists. Early emigrations were haphazard, but later attempts were organised by the *polis* from which they set sail. Such colonies were not dependent upon their mother city and soon became fully independent *poleis*. The scale of the Greek settlements was quite staggering, stretching from Marseilles, in France, to the far shores of the Black Sea. Southern Italy was dominated by Greeks, as was Sicily and the shores of Asia Minor. One of these early colonies was to have an immense role in later Greek history: Byzantium.

It was during the confusing political and social Archaic period that the seeds of later artistic brilliance were sown. When the Dorians came down into Greece their art was mainly concerned with pottery and weapons. It was their contact with Eastern civilisations and the surviving Mycenaeans which stimulated the adoption of new materials and methods. The Greeks quickly learnt how to work in gold, ivory and stone, though styles were slow to develop. The geometric style which had been their hallmark was gradually replaced by the depiction of animals, mythical monsters and floral designs, and the first lifesize, marble statues began to appear.

By the close of the sixth century BC Greece was poised, both politically and culturally, for her most brilliant period. At the same time she was faced with an immensely powerful enemy. The Persian Empire was established in 550 BC on the northern shore of the Persian Gulf and immediately began to expand. In 546 Cyrus II captured Asia Minor and with it the Greek colonies around the shores. The Empire soon embraced land from Libya and Egypt to the Indus Valley in India and from the Arabian Sea to the Caucasus. The Greek colonies rebelled against this foreign domination in 499 BC and called upon mainland Greece for help. The help came in the form of military forces which took and sacked Sardis. But by 494 Darius I of Persia had crushed the rebellion and turned on Greece in a war of revenge.

Four years later a Persian army landed on the Plains of Marathon and was defeated by an Athenian army half its size. So in 480 Xerxes, son of Darius, launched the whole might of the Persian Empire against Greece. More than a thousand ships and hundreds of thousands of men were under the control of Xerxes. Many of the Greek *poleis* united under the leadership of Sparta to fight the Persians, while a few joined Persia in order to pay off old scores. The Persians were delayed for three days by just 300 Spartans, led by their King Leonidas, before bursting through and burning Athens. Soon after this, the Athenian-led fleet crushed that of Persia at Salamis and the invaders retreated into Thessaly. The next year the Greeks marched north to meet the Persians and, although outnumbered, gained a significant victory at Plataea. That same year a Greek expeditionary force in Asia Minor inflicted another defeat upon the Persians, who then retreated from Greece.

As soon as the victory was assured, the *poleis* began to quarrel and the pattern of internecine warfare and intrigue reasserted itself, but the Persian threat remained and would constantly recur. It was against this background of violence that the Geometric art of Archaic Greece was to develop into the Classical creations with which we are familiar. The purpose of art in Ancient Greece was far removed from more modern ideas. The essence of the architecture and the majority of sculptures was that they were to be seen. The famous Parthenon in Athens, for example, was a structural embodiment of the *polis* of Athene. The solid harmony of the architecture reflected that of the city over which it stood. Within the temple was a mighty, 36-foot-tall wooden statue of the goddess Athene, patron of Athens, bedecked with ivory skin, golden armour and coloured eyes. Around the inside of the colonnade runs a frieze depicting the ceremony held every four years, when the people of Athens came to honour their goddess within her temple. The whole building, with its beautiful proportions and magnificent statues, was a celebration of the *polis*. Other statues of gods and goddesses, which today are just statues, were then almost gods. People offered sacrifices to the figures and approached them with trepidation in their hearts.

Architecture first came to the fore with the perfection of the Doric order sometime in the sixth century. Perhaps the best preserved examples of early Doric architecture come from one of the Greek colonies, Paestum in Italy. The gracefully tapered and fluted columns are so perfectly proportioned that even the spaces between them seem to be part of the structure. The Athens Parthenon was the final flowering of this style. The rigidly symmetrical building contains many subtle refinements which illustrate the Greeks' superb mastery of architecture and stonework.

When Athens was burnt by the Persians in 480 BC the temple to Athene was destroyed. So, in 447, with the encouragement of the great statesman Pericles, the Parthenon was begun. It was built of white marble and is 228 feet long by 101 feet wide. Realising that such long, clean lines can lead to optical illusions, the architects compensated by some fine adjustments. The columns are broader half way up their height than elsewhere so as to counteract the illusion that makes straight pillars appear concave. Furthermore, the corner pillars are broader than the others and the spaces between the pillars varies considerably. Perhaps most remarkable is the fact that the pavement upon which the temple is built rises some five inches in a bulge along its length and three inches across its width. All these precise mathematical adjustments were calculated to make the Parthenon appear regular and symmetrical. If it had been built exactly square it would have appeared distorted.

Also on the fortified citadel of Athens, the Acropolis, is the Propylaea, which was built not long after the Parthenon and includes not only the established Doric columns but also those of the newer Ionic style. Ionic, with its slender columns and curved capitals, was more graceful and flowing than the Doric. However, mainland Greece never adopted the Ionic capital for exteriors, preferring to use it for interiors or on smaller temples. Despite this, it was in Athens that many new styles of base were developed for the order. At the same time, in a remote area of the Peloponnese, a temple to Apollo was built which incorporated an entirely new style of column. It is said that the great architect Callimachus was faced by the unsuitability of the Ionic capital for corners and so tried to develop a capital which appeared the same from any angle. The result was the Corinthian style with its curled acanthus leaves and florid lines. This luxurious style was opulent but expensive and difficult to carve so it remained even less popular than the Ionic.

The architecture of Greece has had a profound effect on that of Europe for centuries, so it is perhaps unfortunate that it never extended much beyond the needs of temples and theatres. The styles and ideas were rigidly defined and never reached the variety and diversity of the Romans. Even so, the ideas and theories that the Greeks formulated remained in force until the fall of Rome and were later revived during the Renaissance.

The development of Greek sculpture shows the trail of imagination and invention which was the hallmark of the Greeks. They learnt the art of sculpture from the Egyptians and the people of other Eastern lands, where the human figure was depicted in rigidly traditional style. The object of such Eastern sculpture was to portray the human figure as it actually was rather than as it appeared. The unfortunate result was that although hands, feet, eyes and all other anatomical features were accurately portrayed, the figure was a stilted collection of parts rather than a cohesive whole. The Egyptian statues, from which many stylistic forms were copied, were made more inflexible by symbolising social status by pose. A scribe, for instance, was depicted squatting, while an important official was shown striding purposefully forwards. Archaic Greek sculpture followed the same lines, but it was not long before imagination took hold.

Slowly the sculptors changed the pose of their figures as they began to depict the human figure as it actually appeared. Torsos and hips tilted to one side as weight was taken on one leg and the action gradually became more relaxed. At the same time drapery began to lose its starched stiffness and to mould itself lightly to the figure beneath. It was perhaps the intrusion of sculpture into architecture which really freed the figure from the stilted, frontal pose. Friezes of sculpted figures in high and low relief adorned various parts of temples. The frieze around the colonnade presented the Archaic sculptors with an ideal rectangular space for their stiff figures. The triangular space at the pediments, however, presented problems because of its awkward shape. The first answer found by artists was to place larger figures at the centre of the triangle and smaller ones at the edges. Such a solution was unsátisfactory and before long the idea of depicting a battle scene came into favour. Struggling figures filled the tall central region while the dead and dying conveniently covered the outer regions. Such a design necessitated a rejection of the Archaic pose and the use of far more vigorous figures.

After the defeat of the Persians the true Classical Age began and sculptors took more notice of what they saw. At the same time the very purpose of Greek sculpture pushed it away from complete naturalism. Statues represented gods, and nobody can worship a god with a wart or a squint, so the sculptors aimed to portray the ideal human. The idea spilled over into other forms of sculpture and the art of portraiture was lost.

At Delphi and Olympia statues of the victorious athletes of the sacred games were erected at the temples. Only one of these, a charioteer from Delphi, has survived and reveals the glory of Greek bronzes of the Classical era. Though it is representative of an actual victor, the statue probably bears little resemblance to the athlete; rather it depicts a divinely blessed charioteer of heroic form. The clean lines of the face are smooth and unblemished and the expression serene. At the same time it retains features lost in all too many statues. The eyes are not blank and dull, but are shining with coloured stones, while the hair is lightly gilded, suggesting richness and warmth. A similar work, which has only survived in the form of a later Roman copy, is the *Discus Thrower* by Myron, one of the greatest of Greek sculptors.

As the Classical age progressed, the search for the ideal human spread from the male to the female. The statue of Aphrodite by Praxiteles was so famous that it was one of the most copied statues of antiquity; unfortunately, only copies survive. Praxiteles' other great work *Hermes Carrying the Infant Dionysus* has survived in its original, though damaged, form and shows us the heights that Classical sculpture could reach. In all these works the realistic representation of the human body was advanced far beyond anything else ever created. Unfortunately, the striving for an ideal took away much of the realism. Strong emotion never showed on the faces of gods and heroes for that was not the ideal. Neither did extremes of age intrude into the world of sculpture, babies being as unusual as old men. Such unrealistic realism was slowly disappearing at the end of the Classical period, but the actual change was marked by one of the most successful and amazing periods in Greek history.

In 356 BC a son was born to King Philip II of Macedon. Macedonia was a barbarian kingdom in the eyes of the Greeks, but it had absorbed many aspects of Greek culture and had become distinctly Hellenic. Philip II was an able diplomat and general who was determined to extend the power and prestige of his kingdom. To this end he embarked upon a series of wars and diplomatic intrigues which made Macedonia the dominant power in Greece. In 338 BC an alliance of Athens, Thebes and many smaller *poleis* marched against Philip, determined to defeat the Macedonian army and restore the freedom of the city states. At Chaeronea Philip met the allies and crushed them. That same year Philip called the Congress of Corinth and imposed his will upon Greece. A league was formed of all Greek *poleis* and states, whose democratic decisions were binding on all members. Macedonia remained outside the League of Corinth but retained control of all Greek armies and had effective control of Greece.

Two years later Philip was murdered and his remarkable son came to the throne. For more than a century Greece had hummed with hatred of Persia and more than one man had urged a national war of revenge. With Greece at last united, albeit by force, Alexander, who had been educated by Aristotle, could fulfil the national aim. To achieve this Alexander had inherited from his father the formidable

Macedonian army. With its emphasis on archery and heavy cavalry the army was far removed from the traditional, heavily armoured, infantry hoplite phalanx of the *poleis*. The main battle-winning element was the 2,000-strong Companions, highly trained cavalry whose shock effect few could resist. Even so, Alexander's army had a core of hoplite infantry whose tactical superiority rested on their fourteen-foot pikes, which outreached any other infantry weapon of the time.

In 334 BC Alexander crossed the Dardanelles with just 35,000 troops and began his long march to glory. First of all he visited Troy, the site of an earlier Greek victory in Asia Minor, and then marched upon the Granicus River, today known as the Kocabas. The mighty Persian Empire was governed by local officials known as satraps, and Alexander met the combined forces of three of these at the river. After smashing the Persians Alexander liberated the Greek towns of Asia Minor. The following year Alexander was shown an incredibly complicated knot in Gordium and told that if he could untie it he would rule Asia. Alexander promptly took out his sword and sliced through the problem.

After this exhibition of lateral thinking Alexander marched south, only to find that Darius III had massed the imperial Persian army behind him. At Issus Alexander's skilful use of his troops crushed the Persians and Darius was forced to flee, leaving his family behind him. Resuming his march towards Egypt, Alexander took the Phoenician towns along the coasts of present day Syria, Lebanon and Israel. By early 331 Egypt had fallen to the conqueror. Alexander was crowned as Pharaoh and hailed as the son of Amon, the chief Egyptian god. On the delta of the Nile he founded one of the many cities which he named after himself: Alexandria. Meanwhile, Darius had raised a new army and Alexander marched north to meet it. The armies met east of Nineveh, now in northern Iraq, and Darius suffered complete defeat. Alexander skilfully attacked in oblique order and destroyed his enemy's left wing before turning inwards to complete the destruction.

After capturing the Persian capital of Susa and the palace of Persepolis, Alexander sent the Greek troops home and pushed onwards with his personal forces. He continued beyond the borders of the Persian Empire with seemingly insatiable ambition. In 329 he stood on the northern slopes of the Himalayas and gazed across the great Eurasian steppes whence, seven centuries later, so much suffering would descend on his own country. Here Alexander founded a city which, like all his others, he named Alexandria. The habit of naming cities after national leaders is clearly not dead for the city has been renamed Leninabad by the modern Russian authorities. Other Alexandrias have retained their names, though often in corrupted forms; Kandahar in Afghanistan for example.

In 327 Alexander marched across modern Afghanistan and invaded the Indus Valley. On the banks of the Hydaspes, modern Jhelum, he met the forces of King Porus and forced them to flee. At this point, when Alexander was poised on the edge of India, his loyal troops revolted. They were homesick and refused to march any further. Alexander could do nothing to dissuade them so he returned to Susa. Here he set about organizing his vast conquests and, perhaps, planning fresh campaigns to the west. Before he could accomplish either he died in 323 at the age of 32.

Though the unity of Alexander's empire died with him, his conquests were of vital importance. The empire was divided up by his generals who took the titles of kings and proceeded to establish dynasties and to make war upon each other and their neighbours. Indeed, the Greek kings in India pushed much further east than had Alexander. At the same time they spread the influence of Greek culture from Egypt to India and far beyond their political frontiers. In effect a single economic and, to some extent, cultural sphere was created which reached from the Atlantic to the Indian Oceans. The system was to survive until the fall of Rome seven centuries later and was to have an effect on Western Europe even after that. Of more immediate economic impact were the vast treasures that Alexander captured and released into the economy of the Mediterranean world. At Susa he captured the imperial Persian treasury, which contained 50,000 talents of gold, each talent being roughly equal to 56 pounds.

Back in Greece, the glory and wealth accrued through Hellenising the known world brought peace and prosperity. In its wake came renewed interest in art, which now took a fresh turn. Alexander's assumption of divinity and his generals' kingship brought an interest in portraiture which had been absent before. In turn, this interest led away from the idealised human of Classical sculpture towards a more realistic approach. Fighting figures exhibited genuine emotions of fear, anger and hatred in their struggles, perhaps the most famous example of this work being the *Laocoon* from Rhodes. At the same time old men and babies were accurately portrayed for the first time. Architecture also took a new line, with the more flamboyant Corinthian order becoming increasingly popular and buildings generally becoming more elaborate. Architects began to use the arch and the vault in their works, though such subtleties were in a minority; columns and architraves continuing to be more popular.

At the same time the imposition of royal authority, often from outside Greece, and the influx of foreigners, caused the gradual breakdown of the *polis* as a unit. Trade shifted away from Greece and the cities lost some of their prosperity and wealth, while their governments were beginning to falter and crumble. The decline into which Greece was gradually slipping was not a simple result of the Hellenistic monarchies. The slackening of trade and stagnation of government were evident before Philip II took over Greece, indeed they may have contributed to his success. Lack of prosperity has also been cited as a reason for Alexander's ambitions in the east. The slow process had begun before Alexander, but only became evident after his death.

At the same time that Greece was declining a new power was emerging to the west: Rome. The victorious Roman legions carried Roman domination across Italy, Spain and North Africa before turning on Greece. If Greece was politically in decline it still had a decided cultural advantage over Rome. The colonies in southern Italy had long had an influence on Rome, which had adopted Greek architecture and art. Later Greek sculptures, such as the *Venus de Milo*, were extensively copied in Rome and even the gods of Greece were, to some extent, taken over by the Romans, who gave them Latin names. The contact which Rome had with Greece itself brought about the first flowering of Latin literature, with comedies and epic poems being produced in imitation of Greek models. Furthermore, Greek ideas on justice prevailed in Rome and the city long regarded as barbaric became sophisticated and refined.

Such cultural superiority did not save Greece from the military might of the Italian power. In 200 BC the Roman Republic declared war on Philip V of Macedonia as he was threatening Rhodes, an ally of Rome. Philip was not of the measure of his earlier namesake and lost the war, whereupon Rome declared the independence of Greece. Philip instantly began to prepare for a war of revenge but died in 179. His son Perseus continued his work but by 168 his armies were destroyed. Rome divided Macedonia into four subservient republics which, in 148, became a mere province. Two years later Rome turned upon the very cities which she had declared independent, seizing Sparta and other strategic sites. Faced by military domination, the declining cities mobilised their armies, but could only raise a few men and were overwhelmed. When rebellion broke out in Corinth the Romans burnt the beautiful city to the ground, killed every adult man and sold the women and children into slavery. Greece was quelled.

During the centuries of rule from Rome, Greece itself continued to decline, though Athens and Sparta maintained some of their prosperity. Macedonia, though conquered, remained wealthy enough to produce supplies for wars against the Parthians. During the second century AD a terrible plague swept through the area, further disrupting trade, while the tax burden imposed by Rome stifled efforts at revival. In AD 393 the sacred Olympic Games were banned by Emperor Theodosius I after a history of nearly twelve centuries. The immense religious significance of the games was gone and the pagan culture of Greece was at an end.

By way of contrast, the Greek civilisation was thriving in the islands and colonies. One of the Archaic Greek colonies now moved into a dominant position under a new name. In AD 306 Constantine was declared Emperor by his troops, though it would be almost twenty years before he achieved sole authority. For many years it had been obvious that Rome was no longer a useful capital for the Empire. As a soldier, Constantine moved his capital to the most useful strategic centre: Byzantium. Renaming the city Constantinople, he

moved the apparatus of government to the east and began to build on a lavish scale. Constantinople saw itself as the new Rome, founded on Christian rather than pagan beliefs, and was to maintain itself for a thousand years. As time passed it became increasingly clear that the west was weakening as economic life collapsed and barbarians flooded across the frontiers. In 396 the Empire was officially divided in two, with Greece and the rest of the East being ruled by an increasingly Greek government, known as Byzantine, in Constantinople.

In about 370 the Byzantines became aware of a terrible new threat. Advancing from the Eurasian steppes upon which Alexander had once gazed came the Huns, whose ferocity and ruthlessness were to become legendary. They quickly destroyed the Empire of the Ostrogoths, centred north of the Black Sea. By 380 they had also shattered the Visigoths in Romania and arrived on the frontiers of the Eastern Empire. At first the Byzantines were able to control the barbaric hordes by subtle diplomacy and bribes, but in 434 Attila became King of the Huns. He demanded 700 pounds of gold each year as the price for peace. When the Byzantines failed to pay in 440 he unleashed his warriors.

The Huns achieved their stupendous successes through their complete dominance of the field of battle. Their entire army was mounted and excelled in sweeping envelopments, surprise attacks and equally sudden retreats. They were superb horsemen, being able to bring down men with their bows arrows when riding at full gallop, and could manoeuvre across a field in unison. There can be little wonder that the staid armies of Europe were helpless. But it was not their fighting abilities alone which made the Huns the most feared men in Europe. Their brutality was unparalleled. When the Persians and Romans invaded they came in search of fresh provinces to rule; the Huns came in search of plunder and mayhem. They revelled in destruction and massacred whole populations in the course of their campaigns.

Attila crossed the Danube and destroyed several towns before retiring. In 443 he attacked again and headed straight for the Imperial capital. Within a year he had annihilated the Byzantine army and surrounded the city. But his mounted archers were incapable of storming the walls of Byzantium and Attila left, taking with him nearly three tons of gold and the promise of another ton each year. The Empire lay prostrate and when Attila returned in 447 there was nothing it could do to stop him. The savage hordes of mounted warriors swept down through the Balkans and into Greece. The whole region was devastated as the rampaging armies roamed at will and the Greeks fled before them. Then, suddenly, Attila stopped and turned north in search of fresh plunder in Germany, France and Italy.

North of Lamia Greece had ceased to exist. Proud cities were nothing more than smoking ruins inhabited only by the dead. Crops rotted in the fields because there was nobody left alive to harvest them. The blow dealt to Greece in a single year reverberated for centuries as the country struggled to rebuild its population and wealth.

If Greece itself was devastated, Constantinople, and Greek culture, quickly recovered from the Huns and expanded territorially. In 527 Justinian I came to the throne of Constantinople and ushered in a glorious age for the Greeks. As the successor to the Roman Emperors and the protector of the true Christians against heretics, Justinian saw his duty clearly. He had to rebuild the Roman Empire and conquer the heretic Arians who ruled large areas of Europe. He was brilliantly successful. By the end of his reign the Byzantine Empire stretched from the Black Sea to the Atlantic and Rome was regained.

With the political resurgence came a great artistic revival. Greek culture had survived in the Ionian Islands and the Hellenistic regions and now it came to the fore once more in Constantinople. As time went by the city moved further and further from its Roman origins. Greek became the official language and the whole social, economic and religious emphasis moved towards the east. While the west slipped into barbarism the new Greek Empire maintained the standards and preserved knowledge. It was at Byzantium that so much ancient knowledge and history was preserved, and here that art survived. That is not to say that artistic trends stagnated around Roman or Greek models. Far from it, Christianity had a profound impact and by the turn of the first millennium a completely new style had emerged. The mosaics and paintings of Byzantium were far superior to anything in the west and the buildings they adorned were marvelled at by visitors. Hagia Sophia, the church built by Justinian in the 530s, is a magnificent early example of the distinctive Byzantine church. Domes, cupolas, vaulting and semi-domes proliferate and were to prove a lasting feature of the style. At the same time the Eastern Orthodox Church grew away from Roman Catholicism, a development which angered the west.

The great cultural and artistic brilliance built up by around the year 1200 was soon put in jeopardy. For many years the empire had been dominated by urban civil servants who disliked the brutal side of war. They had refused to maintain the army, preferring to spend money on other, more civilised, projects instead. In 1204 Byzantium reaped the fruits of such policies. The religious split between East and West, together with economic rivalries, brought a western army to the gates of Constantinople at the same time that the empire was threatened by other enemies. The long-neglected army could offer little resistance and the city fell for the first time in over a thousand years.

By the time the westerners finally left in 1259 the empire had been stripped of most of its provinces and of its wealth. For another two centuries Byzantium and the Greek world managed to struggle on against numerous enemies and with depleted resources. But in 1453 the aggressive Ottoman

Turks, led by Mehmed II, laid siege to Constantinople with an army of a quarter of a million men. The defenders could only raise 9,000 troops. The city held out for weeks against the overwhelming odds and the modern cannon of the Turks, but on May 28 it was clear that the end was near. The Emperor, Constantine XI, ordered religious processions to take place and a spectacular Mass was celebrated by the city. That night the Turkish assault began, and on May 29 the Greek Empire perished in a welter of blood, the Emperor himself being killed in the attack.

The long occupation by the Turks brought varying fortunes to the Greeks. At first, life for the ordinary peasant was probably little different from before; Christianity was tolerated and taxes were moderate. However, only Muslims were allowed to hold public office and Christians were treated as second class citizens. In time, the Ottoman administration began to crumble and lawlessness became rife. It was against this background of weakened authority and disorder that the Greeks rebelled in 1821. They quickly gained local success, capturing Athens, Thebes and Missolonghi, but the Greeks were far from united and civil war broke out. It was only help from European powers which stopped the Turks retaking Greece, and in 1832 the Ottomans recognised Greece as an independent kingdom. The modern state of Greece was born.

The Greece of today is far removed from the land of the *poleis*, even from that of Byzantium. Time has wrought many changes upon the native culture, while invaders and immigrants have brought their own styles and traditions. Through all the political upheavals that have befallen Greece, the Greek language has survived, but 3,000 years have changed it considerably from the Greek of Homer. Perhaps more important are the local variations of speech which have grown up in the geographically fragmented land of Greece. Tsakonian, which is spoken in the mountains of the eastern Peloponnese, is closest to the original Doric language. By contrast, most of the Peloponnese speaks a more modern dialect. Other important dialects, many of which are unintelligible to each other, are found in northern Greece, around Athens, Crete and the islands around Rhodes. Out of such confusion arose demotic Greek, a form which is spoken in most large cities and can be understood by most Greeks. Not content with one standard language the Greeks have introduced another, the Katharevusa. Katharevusa came about as a nineteenth century effort to standardise Greek along Classical lines. It is used today in newspapers and government circles, but rarely elsewhere.

Something which is seen all over Greece is the *taverna*. In this unique institution the Greeks will drink, talk, dance, eat or simply relax. They serve as a focus for the local community and have far more to do with modern Greece than the Parthenon. The wines and cuisine are uncompromisingly local and Greek in character. Greek cooking, true to its Byzantine heritage, is more eastern than European. Olive oil is the dominant cooking fat, as it has been for centuries, which gives the cuisine a distinctive flavour. Around the coasts and on the islands fish is popular enough to be almost a staple, and is cooked superbly. Shellfish, such as prawns and crayfish, are best in the simple sauce of oil and lemon juice which is so popular. Octopus and squid, on the other hand, are more often stewed in wine to bring out their subtle flavour. Meat dishes are not the speciality of Greece, though Greek spring lamb is the best in the world and the poultry is full of flavour.

Greek drinks vary from the well known *ouzo* to wines whose names are as elusive as their quality. *Ouzo* is the most popular aperitif in Greece. It is served in thimblefuls in the countryside but in the towns it is poured more generously, often mixed with water. Amongst the islands the sweet *citro* from Naxos is more in favour. The most Greek of Greek wines are those which are flavoured with resin, and these take some getting used to for connoisseurs of wine.

The land which modern Greeks inhabit is both similar to and different from the Greece which the ancients knew. The same hills rise above the same olive-grove-covered plains, but the cities are far removed from the *poleis* of the Dorians. Athens was the cultural centre of Greece in the days of Pericles and is now the capital city of the modern nation.

When Kekrops established his city on the Acropolis, Poseidon and Athene contended for patronage of the city. Poseidon created the horse, but Athene produced the olive tree which was deemed to be of more practical use and the city was named Athens in her honour. The olive spread out across the Plain of Attica, becoming the agricultural basis of Athens. Just two centuries ago Athens was little more than a village perched on the slopes of the Acropolis. Its designation as capital and its strategic position brought it fresh prosperity and population. Today, the city suburbs have spread out across the plain which was once covered with shady olive groves.

The modern city has, with Piraeus, become the great trading and manufacturing centre of the nation. The port is an important factor in the city's economic life, as are chemical works, cloth manufacturing, distilling and various other industries. With these industries paying wages three times higher than the national average, it is hardly surprising that people have flocked to the city. The population of the conurbation is rapidly approaching four million; over a third of the national total. Such a population has brought more than half the nation's cars, lorries and buses to Athens. Pollution has, therefore, become a terrible problem. The fumes have eaten into the grand stonework of the Acropolis monuments, forcing the Greeks to remove many sculptures to special museums. The buildings, of course, cannot be moved and the gradual crumbling of these fine works is a pressing problem. The pollution has all but destroyed another famous sight in Athens. The city has long been

known as the 'violet-crowned' because of its spectacular sunsets. As the sun sinks in the west the slopes of Mount Hymettus glow with a soft, violet light. Suddenly, the delicate suffusion vanishes and the city is plunged into night. These days the beautiful effect is only seen when a north wind blows the grey cloud of fumes away.

As the capital of Greece, Athens was the centre of Greek learning and power throughout the Classical period. A millenium earlier the true centre of the Aegean civilisation had been thriving on Crete, largest of the Greek islands. The Cyclopean walls of Mycenae have survived the centuries, but in their day they were crude compared to the edifices of Crete. The civilisation of the island had been gradually developing since the close of the Stone Age when a new people arrived, perhaps from Anatolia. This new civilisation centred around palaces. At first there were numerous small palaces, suggesting a proliferation of independent states. As the centuries passed the smaller palaces were deserted while the larger palaces became grander and more splendid, suggesting that power was increasingly concentrated. In time the island may have been united under the king known to legend as Minos. The fine civilisation eventually fell beneath the onslaught of volcanic eruption and foreign invasion centuries before the Dorians moved into Greece. Foreign invaders came to the island again in May 1941, during the Second World War, when the island was the scene of a massive landing by German airborne troops. Though the assault was successful it proved so costly that the Germans never employed such tactics again.

The island itself has changed remarkably little over the centuries. Industry has made few inroads into the economic scene and three-quarters of the population lives outside the main towns. The beautiful climate, which no doubt encouraged the early civilisations, now plays its part in the growing of olives, grapes, melons, peaches, bananas and other fruits for which the island is famous. A more recent development dependent on the climate is the tourist industry. Roads are being built all over the island in order to open up the more remote regions. The north coast already has several fine resorts along its beaches and the south coast is rapidly catching up. Despite the development of such beach towns it is the remains of the ancient palaces which are still the distinctive Cretan attraction.

Crete lies at the southern end of the Aegean Sea, but it is far from being the only island in the crystal blue waters of the area. There are well over a thousand islands in the Aegean, each with a name heavy with romance and history. Some of the islands are vital to the Greek economy, but two millennia ago the most important island was one of the smallest.

Delos covers less than two square miles and is virtually uninhabited, yet it contains some of the most extensive ruins in Greece. From the earliest times the tiny island was considered holy by the Greeks as the birthplace of Apollo and Artemis. The temples, sanctuaries, oracle and festivals were so sacred that the Persians deliberately avoided Delos when on their way to Marathon. The festival began when the sacred ship arrived from Athens and a solemn procession took place to the sound of a sacred song. Athletics and musical competitions followed, together with a sacred dance, plays and banquets. The oracle of Apollo at Delos was considered second only to that of Delphi and had a profound effect on men's lives. In 88 BC Delos was taken by troops of the Hellenistic monarch Mithradates VI of Pontus as part of his desperate struggle against expansionist Rome. The town was destroyed and never recovered.

From the peak of Mount Kynthos, above the five Archaic stone lions of Delos, a superb view of the Cyclades is gained. These islands gained their name because they seem to circle around the holy island. The sparkling blue of the Aegean is interrupted by a series of bare, rocky islands, all of which have archaeological interest. Of more immediate importance is the fact that they are in the forefront of the tourist industry. The large scale development of some of the islands has robbed the beach towns of the charm which first attracted visitors. Inland, however, or on some of the smaller islands, the simple, rural atmosphere is still to be found.

To the east of the Cyclades is one of the few Greek islands whose fame rests as much on medieval events as on ancient splendour. Myth maintains that Rhodes was named in honour of a nymph who was loved by Helios, the guardian god of the island. Others maintain that the name is derived from *erod*, the Phoenician word for snake, pointing to the fact that even today farmers wear tough boots as protection against the venomous snakes. In 304 BC the city survived a long siege by Demetrius Poliocrates, later King of Macedonia, and the jubilation was akin to that accompanying the Relief of Mafeking. Being Greeks, the citizens of Rhodes celebrated by erecting a statue of their patron god Helios. What made this statue the wonder of Greece was the fact that it was over 100 feet tall. The Colossus was made of bronze, reinforced with iron and stone, and was the work of Chares of Lindus. The statue fell during an earthquake in 225 BC, but remained intact until AD 653, when the Arabs captured Rhodes and melted the statue down.

The island erupted into history centuries later during the Crusades. Inspired by the vision of recapturing Holy Jerusalem from the unbelieving Saracens, the knights of Christendom descended upon Palestine. For many years the onslaught of the Christians was successful and they captured large areas of the Holy Land. By the close of the thirteenth century, however, the forces of Islam had the upper hand and the crusaders were on the retreat. One of the orders of knights which had fought in the Holy Land was the Knights of Saint John of Jerusalem, the Hospitallers. In 1309 the Hospitallers took over Rhodes from the Byzantine Empire and turned it into a massive fortress. Being so close to

the mainland of Asia Minor, Rhodes was a target for the followers of Allah. In 1444 the Sultan of Egypt led his forces against Rhodes, only to be defeated. Thirty-six years later Mehmed II, the conqueror of Constantinople, led 70,000 of his best troops against Rhodes. In turn this force was repulsed by the defenders.

In 1522 Sultan Suleyman the Magnificent landed on Rhodes with well over 100,000 men and laid siege to the city. Even this mighty force was not enough and the conflict ground into a bloody stalemate. Eventually the Knights of Saint John agreed to leave Rhodes on condition that they left with honour. The Sultan was only too glad to agree and the impregnable fortress of Rhodes was handed over. The final trial of strength between the Turks and the Knights came in 1565 at Malta, when the Christians withstood another terrible siege. Today, this order of knights still survives, one of its better known branches being the Saint John's Ambulance Corps. If the Colossus has disappeared the fortifications of the Knights of Saint John certainly have not. The Old City is encircled by the walls which were reconstructed after an earthquake in 1481. The massive defenses are dotted with towers and pierced by numerous firing loops which covered every inch of the ditch in front of them. Within the defenses are still found the 'inns' where the knights lived, and many other reminders of the town's heroic past.

To the west of the Cyclades lies the Peloponnese, perhaps the most Greek area of the mainland. Almost an island, this peninsula is linked to Europe only by the Isthmus of Corinth, and even that link is now broken by a canal. The mountainous peninsula has some of the most majestic scenery in Greece; wooded slopes contrasting with bare hills in the hot, still air.

The central region of the peninsula, Arcadia, has retained more of its original character than many other regions. For the Romantics the region was an idyllic area of simple shepherds and shepherdesses, but in Classical times it was renowned for its backwardness and cruelty. Neither image is really true of today's Arcadia. The air of rusticity and backwardness is dispelled near Tropea, where the river Ladonas has been dammed as part of the nation's largest hydroelectric scheme. The lake fills the winding valley behind the dam and is dominated by the peaks of the mountains, giving it the atmosphere of a Norwegian fiord. From the lake the waters gush along a six-mile-long underground tunnel to the power station. The roads through the region offer perhaps the most scenic driving in Greece, though a sheer, thousand-foot drop can be a little unnerving.

In antiquity the most powerful *polis* on the peninsula was undoubtadly Sparta, which stands on the Plain of Laconia. The small, modern city of some 14,000 citizens dates only from 1834, when the newly independent Greece felt obliged to re-found this great city. Its modest prosperity is founded on the local orange and olive groves and its architecture is uninspiring. To the north, however, stand the ruins of ancient Sparta and a statue to that epitome of Spartan ideals: King Leonidas.

The whole society of Sparta, formulated by the lawgiver Lycurgus in the Archaic period, was geared for war. The purpose of the Helots, the lowest caste, was simply to farm the estates and produce enough food to keep the army in the field. The Perioikoi were free men but were required to serve as hoplites in time of war. It was the upper caste who ruled Sparta, but they did not have an easy life. Weak babies were left on the slopes of Taiyetos to die, while the stronger sons were taken from their families when seven years old and placed in military training camps. The discipline was notoriously strict and harsh, but when he joined the army at twenty years of age the Spartan had no equal in Greece. For years Sparta needed no city walls because its army was so formidable that no enemy dared attack the city itself. The heroic stand of Leonidas and his 300 hoplites, who died to a man at Thermopylae, was the example to which young Spartiates aspired.

If Sparta was the military centre of the Peloponnese, the cultural and religious centre lay to the northwest, at Olympia. The great festival of games and arts that was held here every four years first took place in 776 BC and counted Apollo and Heracles amongst its earliest victors. Originally the games consisted of only one event, a foot race the length of the stadium. The purpose of this trial was not to find the best athlete but to discover upon whom the gods had bestowed divine strength and skill. In time the programme was extended to include javelin, boxing, long jump, chariot racing and a host of other events. The festival was punctuated by the appearance of great poets and historians who recited their works to the crowd. The audience witnessed a more spectacular interruption in 364 BC when a full-scale battle between the armies of Pisa and Arcadia took place nearby and spilled over into the sacred enclosure. Fortunately, both sides recognised the sacred truce which protected athletes and spectators and only massacred each other!

Originally only Greek men and boys could compete, but political domination from Rome opened the games to outsiders. In AD 69 Emperor Nero competed in the chariot race and music contests. Despite falling off his chariot twice, Nero won all his events, which surprised nobody. Victors were allowed to erect statues of themselves at Olympia and by the year 1 there were more than three thousand such monuments. After the games were banned by Theodosius, the buildings soon decayed and the stones were taken for new buildings, an earthquake in AD 551 adding to the destruction. The importance of the games to the ancient Greeks was immense and today their revived form is increasingly dominant in modern-day sport.

The third great centre of the ancient Peloponnese was luxury-loving Corinth. Corinth was one of the oldest and largest *poleis* in Greece, originating in pre-Doric times and having a peak population of a third of a million. The dominance of Corinthian commerce during the Archaic period was unquestioned, with Corinthian goods being distributed throughout the Mediterranean lands. The wealth thus created did not lead to military success, as in Sparta, nor to cultural excellence, as in Athens. The Corinthians turned to pleasure. It was no accident that the chief temple was dedicated to Aphrodite and staffed by a thousand sacred prostitutes, nor that the most flamboyant style of architecture is named for the city. After the destruction of the Greek city by the Romans, a new colony of Latins was established on the site. Once again the city became famous for frivolity and pleasure even amongst the decadent Romans. After the devastating earthquake of AD 551 decline set in and the city had to be refounded in 1858. The luxury and hedonism of days gone by have not, however, reappeared.

The cities that today dominate the Peloponnese are not those that earned fame in antiquity. Kalamata dominates the south, with a population of 50,000. The city first entered history as a Byzantine centre and in 1821 was the centre of the revolution which led to Greek independence. Today it is an important outlet for the olives, currants, figs and citrus fruits of the Peloponnese. Patrai, on the Gulf of Corinth, is the third city of Greece and an important port. The three villages of Patrai joined together in the earliest days of the Dorians, but its great days did not begin until the ninth century AD. Its population of over 100,000 is engaged in a variety of trades, but principally in the export and processing of agricultural produce.

On the north coast of the Gulf of Corinth stands Delphi. The fame of Delphi does not rest upon its buildings nor its commercial activity, for Delphi was the seat of the Oracle of Apollo. Pilgrims with questions had to sacrifice an animal and wait while the priestess sat on a tripod over a chasm in the ground and chewed laurel leaves to receive the answers from Apollo. From the earliest times the power and veracity of this oracle was recognised far beyond Greece. Kings and governments came to Delphi to learn their future before embarking on projects. These pronouncements were often ambiguous or even cryptic. Byzas, for example, was told to found his colony 'opposite the city of the blind'. Deciding that the inhabitants of Chalcedon were blinded by the fertility of their own soil, Byzas settled on the north shore of the Bosphorus and thus founded Byzantium. During the Persian wars the Oracle declared that 'sons of men will be devoured at sea'. The great naval victory of Salamis followed and the Greeks hailed the prophecy as fulfilled, but a Persian victory would have justified the Oracle just as firmly.

Beyond Mount Parnassus stands Lamia, near the Gulf of Euboea. This lively market town is best distinguished by the numerous storks' nests which adorn the roofs. To the south of the town is the Pass of Thermopylae and to the north the less well known Fourka Pass. Here, in 1897, Crown Prince Constantine was forced into a similar position to Leonidas when he commanded the Greek army in a last stand against superior Turkish forces. Unlike Leonidas, Constantine survived the battle and became King of the Hellenes in 1913.

North of the Fourka Pass stretches the fertile Plain of Thessaly, which has long been one of the richest areas of Greece. The region takes its name from the Thessalians, a Doric tribe which moved into the region around 1200 BC. These people were on the edge of the mainstream of Greek culture and pursued a divergent course, even to the extent of siding with Persia in 480 BC. When the Huns invaded in AD 447 Thessaly felt the full force of their savagery. Those who did not flee south were butchered, and as a distinct group the Thessalians were destroyed. In the centuries following the invasion of the Huns the area was repopulated by Greeks filtering north and non-Greeks moving south. The Greeks did not always predominate and in the 13th century the area was known as Great Walachia. Even today villages of Walachians can be found across the plain, a reminder that the effects of Attila's hordes are still to be felt.

Since AD 300 Larissa has been the capital of Thessaly and remains so today. It serves principally as a centre for the agricultural wealth of Thessaly and produces silk and *ouzo* of the best quality. At the western edge of Thessaly, where the Pinios flows down from the mountains, rise the most famous monasteries in Greece. The communities of Meteora stand atop isolated crags which rise as much as 1,800 feet from the plain. They were constructed centuries ago by holy men wishing to escape from the pressures of the world and this they certainly achieved in their dramatic retreats. At first the only access to the buildings was by way of baskets hauled up on ropes, but steps were later hacked from the rock. Most of the monasteries have fallen into disuse, but the four largest are still thriving religious centres.

In northern Thessaly rises the majestic mountain which the Classical Greeks considered the edge of Greece and the abode of the gods: Olympus. The mountain reaches to a height of 9,570 feet and is capped by snow for half the year. It was here that the gods were believed to live their all-too-human lives with all their intrigues and affaires.

Epirus, the region of northwestern Greece, has long been considered the most conservative, and occasionally backward, region of Greece. During the Classical period the region was engaged in the kind of inter-tribal warfare which the *poleis* had abandoned centuries earlier. Alexander's mother came from Epirus, but the region did not really become important until Pyrrhus came to the throne in 307 BC. This king resisted Roman expansion and led his army to Italy, where Rome was most vulnerable. Pyrrhus twice defeated the Romans but suffered such disastrous casualties that he declared 'one more such victory and we have lost'. The term Pyrrhic victory thus entered the language of Western Europe.

Even today Epirus is a mountainous land which is often difficult to traverse. Winding mountain roads link the villages and towns where the traditional peasant life continues. Tourism has not really reached this part of Greece, for while the mountains and isolated lakes are picturesque and charming, the climate is distinctly chilly and unwelcoming.

Macedonia was considered by the Greeks to be almost a barbarian country, despite the fact that the inhabitants spoke Greek and had absorbed much Greek culture. Even after Phillip II of Macedon had amalgamated the *poleis* into the League of Corinth his kingdom was looked upon as inferior. In many ways Macedonia is different from the rest of Greece; it lies beyond the mountainous barrier of Olympus and its fertile land is part of a valley which extends deep into Yugoslavia. Even the wet and varied climate links the region with the Balkans rather than the Mediterranean. The population here was even more mixed than in Thessaly and this led to the thorny Macedonian Question in the early years of this century.

Macedonia was claimed by Greece, Serbia and Bulgaria, each basing its claim on the population of the region. It did in fact belong to the Ottomans, but in 1912 the three claimants marched on the Turks. The same Crown Prince Constantine who had defended Fourka marched through the passes of the Olympus Range and inflicted a series of defeats on the Turks. Having expelled the Turks, the three allies fell out and went to war with each other, the result being that Macedonia was divided into three. The mixed population soon sorted itself out and now the people of Greek Macedonia are mainly Greek.

Thessaloniki, the second greatest city in Greece, is located on the coast of Macedonia and is also the nation's second most important port. It was founded in 315 BC in honour of a sister of Alexander the Great and has continued to prosper ever since. Such prosperity has made it a tempting target for invaders and the city passed through many hands before returning to Greece in 1912. The port handles a wide variety of raw material imports, which are then used by the thriving industrial area before being re-exported. Despite the presence of this large, sophisticated city, the hinterland is surprisingly rural and traditional in outlook. Amongst the Macedonian mountains the life of the peasant has continued little changed for centuries.

The same homogeneity of population is not true of Thrace, the easternmost area of mainland Greece. The Turks who mingled with the Greek population in this region were not expelled after 1923 for the Turkish government allowed Greeks to remain in Constantinople. As a result this is the most Eastern in flavour of all the Greek regions in its lifestyle, cuisine and character but at the same time it is an essential part of the nation which was the cradle of Western Civilisation.

Fresco in a Byzantine church in the Agora, Athens.

ΟΑΙ
Ο

ΚΗΡΙΛΟ(Ν)

17

Facing page: the fluted pillars of the Parthenon, built entirely of Pentelic marble, stand at the highest point of the Acropolis of Athens. Above: Mount Lycabettus rises sheer from the centre of Athens, and is topped by the chapel of St George. Overleaf: below the Parthenon lie the ruins of the Odeon of Herodes Atticus (left), a wealthy public benefactor of the 2nd century AD, who built the theatre as a memorial to his dead wife. The Propylaea (right) forms a magnificent entrance way to the Acropolis or 'upper city', extending for 150 feet across the whole of its western front.

From the Propylaea the Sacred Way led to the Parthenon (above left, above and facing page), the temple of the virgin goddess Athene. Built during the golden Periclean age of Athenian democracy, in the 5th century BC, the design of the Parthenon was drawn up by the architect Ictinus, and its sculptural decoration assigned to Pheidias, the greatest sculptor of the time. Ictinus and his collaborators created the new temple as a balanced, Doric structure, softened by containing not a single straight line of any length. The temple's fine exterior sculptures, originally brightly coloured, recounted the history of Athene. The Ionic Temple of Athene Nike (left and overleaf, left) adjoins the Propylaea, and was built to commemorate Greek victories over the Persians, in the 5th century BC. Overleaf: (right) seen from the Acropolis, the ancient Agora, or marketplace, fronts the modern city of Athens.

Facing page: the interior of the Parthenon, showing the *sekos* or temple proper raised two steps above the level of the surrounding colonnade. Above: the Acropolis, with the Odeon of Herodes Atticus on its lower slopes, and the Propylaea and the Parthenon built above white limestone outcrops. Overleaf: the octagonal Tower of the Winds (left), on the western slope of the Acropolis, was built in the 1st century BC as a public hydraulic clock and weather-vane. The frieze depicts the inscriptions and figures of the eight winds into which the compass was divided. (Right) the Parthenon.

Previous pages: the harbour at Hydra, the only town on the long, narrow island of Hydra, off the
Peloponnese. Above: the early 4th century Doric Tholos, or rotunda, at Marmaria in ancient Delphi.
The paved Sacred Way (facing page) leads to the Temple of Apollo, whose priestess voiced the
prophesies of the great Delphic oracle of Apollo. Overleaf: (left) the Temple of Apollo, and (right)
the Theatre, built in the 4th century BC, above the Temple of Apollo, Delphi.

Facing page: the well-preserved Stadium at Delphi, where the Pythian games, dedicated to the worship of Apollo, were held in the September of every fourth year. Above: fluted Doric columns of the Temple of Apollo. Overleaf: (left) the 5th-century-BC Temple of Poseidon, built overlooking the cliffs at Cape Sounio (right), the southernmost point of Attica.

Above: twelve Doric columns remain standing at the Temple of Poseidon, Cape Sounio. Facing page:
fishing boats moored in the harbour of Aegina, capital of Aegina island in the Saronic Gulf.
Overleaf: the Doric temple of the goddess Aphaia, among the mountains on the east coast of Aegina,
is the best-preserved temple in the islands.

Local fishing boats and visiting pleasure cruisers fill the small harbour of Tourkolimano (facing page), and the circular harbour of Zea (above), at Piraeus, the port of Athens. Overleaf: (left) the steep, terraced village of Langadia, in the Arcadian mountains, and (right) the view towards Galatas, on the Peloponnese mainland.

Above: a fertile valley floor in Olympia, farmed in small, intensively cultivated fields. Facing page:
Lefkokhori, above the gorge of the River Lousios, lies west of Langadia in the mountains of Acadia. Built in
the 6th century BC, the Temple of Apollo (overleaf, left) was all that survived the destruction of ancient
Corinth by the Romans in 146 BC. Overleaf: (right) the citadel of Acrocorinth, above the ancient town.

Above: the seven Doric columns of the Temple of Apollo, beyond the ruins of the Roman town of Corinth.
The Canal of Corinth (facing page) connects the Ionian with the Aegean sea, and was completed in 1893.
Overleaf: (left) the remains of a colonnade, and (right) fallen columns, at Olympia, where the
quadrennial games were held, first in honour of the goddess Hera, and then of Zeus.

Fourth-century-BC Epidauros, on the east coast of the Peloponnese, was dedicated to the cult of the physician-god Asklepios, and became a fashionable spa and medical centre as well as a place of worship. Above: the foundations of the Tholos, and (facing page) the Theatre, at Epidauros. The Theatre, best preserved of all Greek theatres, can seat 14,000 spectators along its 55 tiers. Overleaf: (left) the steep, rocky peninsula south of Nafplio, at the head of the Argolic Gulf, and (right) a more gentle coastline.

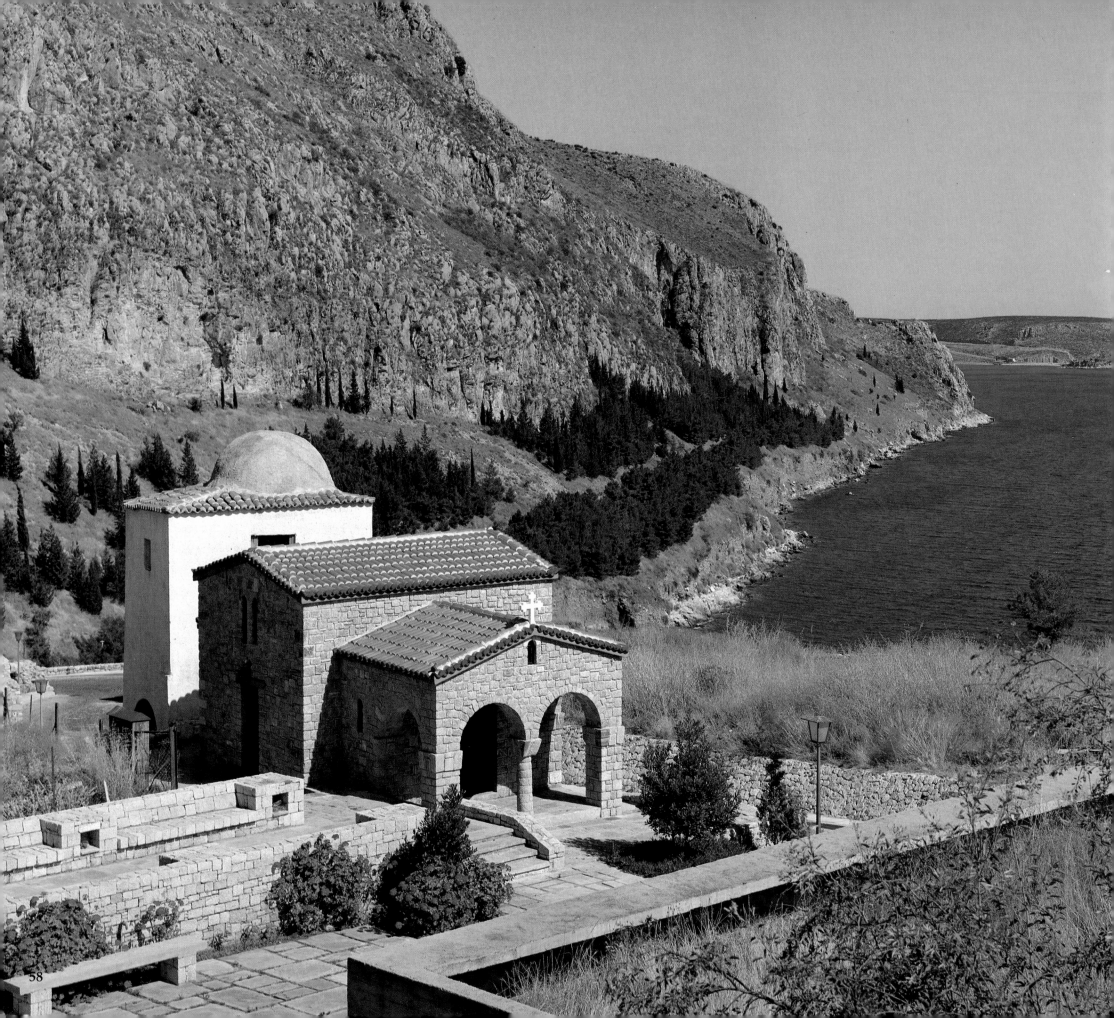

The coastal towns of New Epidauros (left), and Methoni (bottom left). Below: Xenia beach, and (bottom and facing page) the Venetian island-fort of Bourdzi, both at Nafplio. Overleaf: (left) Parga, and (right) Skiathos town.

The fortifications at Methoni (above), in the Peloponnese, were built after the city was assigned to Venice in 1204. Facing page: beach at Edipsos, on the island of Evia. Overleaf: (left) a causeway leads to Vlaherna monastery, and small boats cross to the islet of Pondikonisi, 'Mouse Island', off Corfu. (Right) the fishing village of Limni, on the Evripos, which separates Evia from the Boeotian mainland.

Previous pages: the holiday resort of Parga, in northwestern Greece. Facing page: broom flowers above the villages of Vatonies and Alimatades, north of Paleokastritsa on the island of Corfu. The Ionic rotunda (above) was built on the esplanade of Corfu town in honour of Sir Thomas Maitland, the island's first Lord High Commissioner. Beyond the esplanade lies the old Venetian fort. Overleaf: (left) Corfu sunset, and (right) sunrise over Corfu town harbour.

The tall houses of old Corfu town, (below, bottom and facing page) were once enclosed by city walls. Right and bottom right: gardens in Corfu town. Overleaf: the bays of Paleokastritsa, on Corfu's west coast.

Narrow streets in old Corfu town (below), Sinarades (right), and Aghios Deka (bottom right). Facing page: vines and whitewashed steps, Corfu. Overleaf: (left) sunset at Kaiser's Mount, and (right) rainclouds over Corfu's coastline.

Previous pages: (left) ferries in the harbour, Corfu town, and (right) Mirtiotissa Beach, on Corfu's mountainous west coast. Facing page: the nunnery of Agios Stephanos, and (above) Agios Varlaam, against the Pindos Mountains at Meteora, Thessaly. Most of the precariously-placed monasteries of Meteora originated as 14th-century hermitages, safe from conflicts between the emperors of Trikala and Byzantium over ownership of the fertile valley floor. Overleaf: the white, cubic houses of Mykonos, main town and port of Mykonos island in the Aegean.

Above: the harbour and whitewashed houses of the port of Mykonos, where colour is only permitted on
doors, shutters and the red cupolas of churches (facing page and overleaf, right). Overleaf: (left)
round, thatched windmills above Mykonos town.

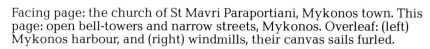

Facing page: the church of St Mavri Paraportiani, Mykonos town. This page: open bell-towers and narrow streets, Mykonos. Overleaf: (left) Mykonos harbour, and (right) windmills, their canvas sails furled.

Left: hand-crafted tourist goods, (top left) fishing boats, and (above) octopuses drying, Mykonos. Top: 'Venice', a row of old houses on the seafront (facing page) in Mykonos town.

Facing page: Thira, main town of Thira island (Santorini). Below and bottom: the arcade of the cathedral, Thira. Right and bottom right: churches on Thirassia, splintered off Thira island by volcanic action in 236 BC.

Previous page: (left) the Sacred Way at ancient Thira, and (right) Thira and the steep path to Skala Thira. The fishing village of Naoussa (top right and facing page) lies on the northeastern shore of Paros, in the Cyclades. Above: a church in the town of Paros, and (right) a team of mules, used to thresh corn, Paros. Overleaf: (left) the harbour at Iraklio, the main town of Crete. The tight-packed village of Plomari (right), Lesbos, produces the island's ouzo.

Below: the Propylaeum and the Horns of Consecration at the Minoan site of Knossos, Crete. Facing page: the Palace, (right) the throne room, and (bottom) giant pithoi, at Knossos. Bottom right: giant pithoi at Iraklio. Overleaf: (left) the plateau of Lasithi, and (right) Agios Nikolaos, Crete.

Previous pages: (left) the north end of Samaria Gorge, and (right) the nearby village of Laki, in Crete's White Mountains. Facing page: Skiathos town, on the thickly-wooded island of Skiathos. Top: Lalaria beach, Skiathos town, and (above) fishing boats at Spetses. Top right: the red-tiled roofs of Plomarion, Lesbos, and (right) white, cubic houses in Naxos town, Naxos.

Previous pages: (left) canvas-sailed windmills, and (right) a mountain road between Tripoli and
Argos in the Peloponnese. Facing page and overleaf right: Pythgorio, on the island of Samos in the
Aegean, and (above) Samos town, seen from Vathi, the upper town. The island of Symi (overleaf, left)
in the Dodecanese Islands, is almost encircled by the mountains of the Turkish mainland. **117**

Above: remains of the 4th-century-BC Temple of Athene within the Acropolis at Lindos, Rhodes, where a temple to the goddess has stood since at least the 10th century BC. Facing page: the fortified Acropolis and the village of Lindos, founded as one of the three ancient cities of Rhodes by Dorian invaders in the 11th century BC. Overleaf: (left) Rhodes' Government House, and (right) the bronze deer at the entrance to Mandraki Harbour, Rhodes town.

In 1306 the chief admiral of the Byzantine Empire sold Rhodes island to the military Order of Knights of St John of Jerusalem. They fortified it heavily, building the battlemented walls of the old city (previous pages, left). Previous pages: (right) part of the large Doric stoa on the Acropolis at Lindos, and (facing page) ruins of the residential quarter of Kamiros, another of the ancient Dorian cities of Rhodes. Top left: the medieval street of the Knights, Rhodes town, and (left) three windmills on the mole of Aghios Nikolaos, Mandraki Harbour. Above: the steps of the Doric stoa, and (overleaf) the entrance to the Knights' castle, both part of Lindos Acropolis, Rhodes.